Nola the Nurse®

Preschool Activity Book

Volume 1

by Dr. Scharmaine L. Baker NP

Illustrated by Marvin Alonso

A DrNurse
Publishing House

New Orleans, Louisiana

COPYRIGHT ©2016 by Dr. Scharmaine L. Baker and its licensors.
All rights reserved.

No part of this book may be reproduced or transmitted in any form or by any means, electronic or mechanical, including photocopy, recording, or by any information storage and retrieval system without the written permission of the publisher or author except where permitted by law.

For information address A DrNurse Publishing House
2475 Canal Street, Suite 105, New Orleans, La. 70119
www.NolatheNurse.com

ISBN-13: 978-1-945088-05-6
ISBN-10: 1-945088-05-6

Author Contact info:
DrBakerNP@NolaTheNurse.com

www.DrBakerNP.com
www.NolaTheNurse.com

Match the picture to its correct outline.

Tick [✓] the missing part of the picture.

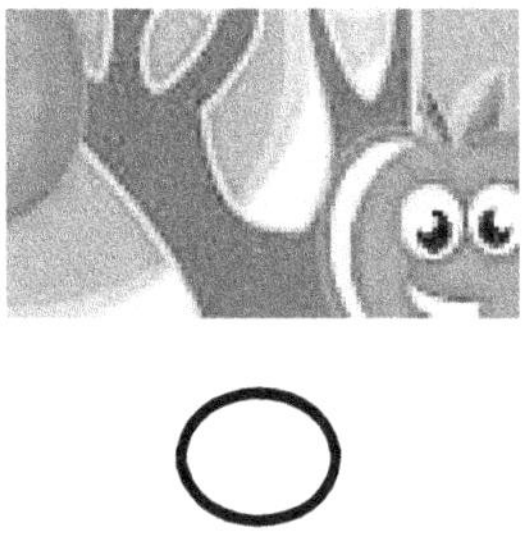

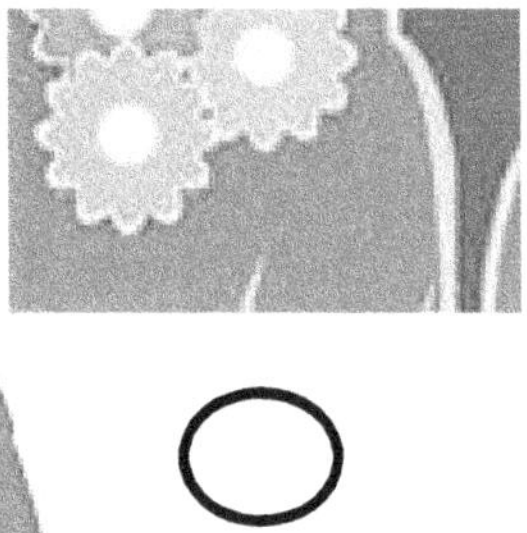

Help the fox to eat her food.

Find five differences between these two images.

www.NolaTheNurse.com

Make your own house by using the dots.

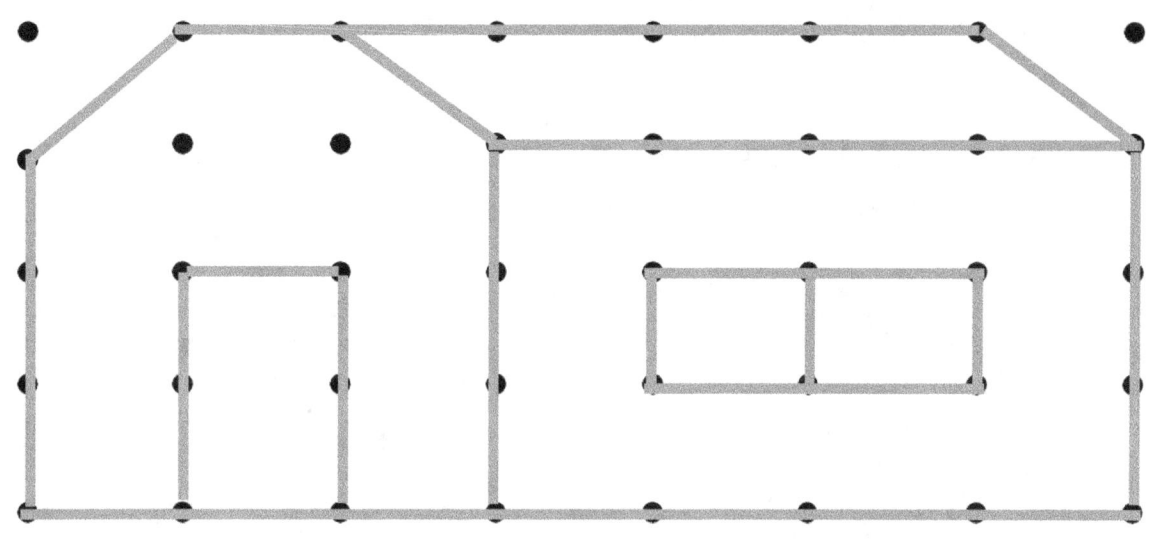

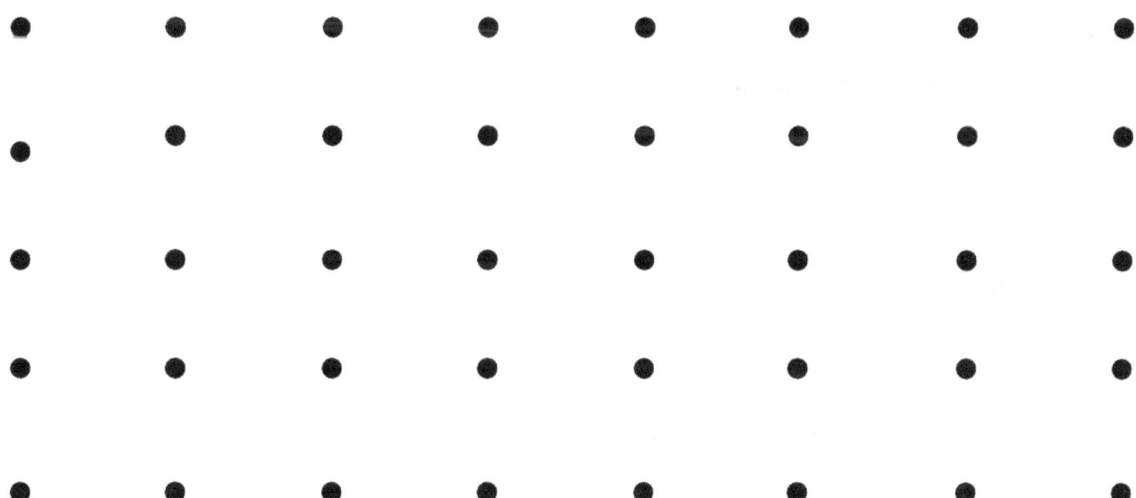

www.NolaTheNurse.com

Rearrange the jumbled pieces of the given picture.

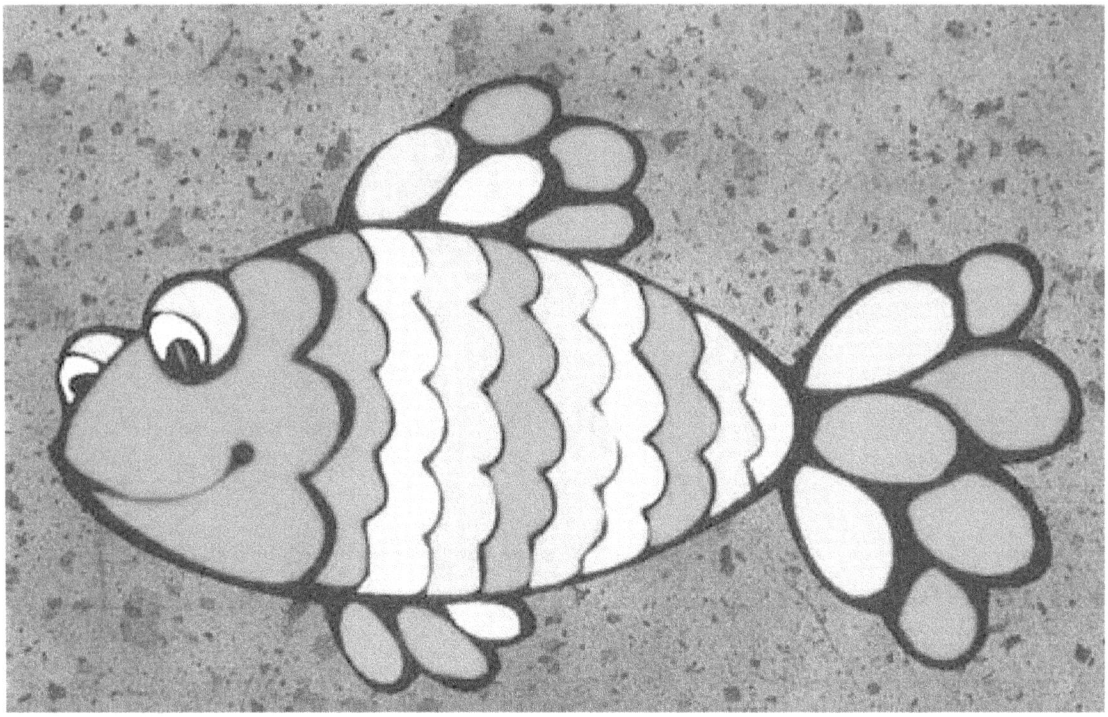

A 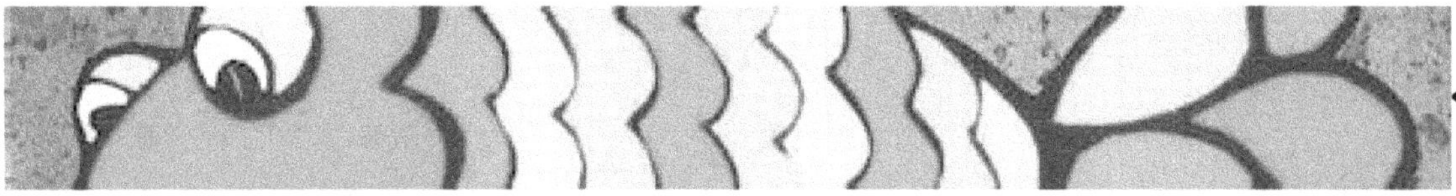

B 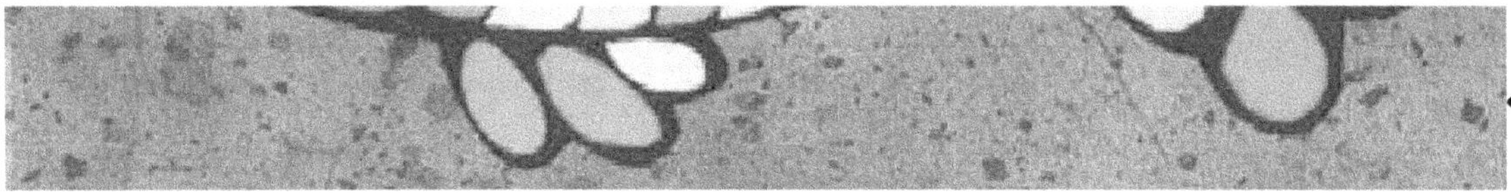

C 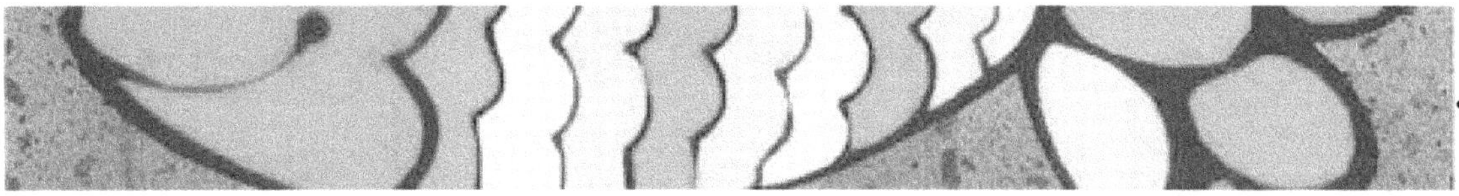

D 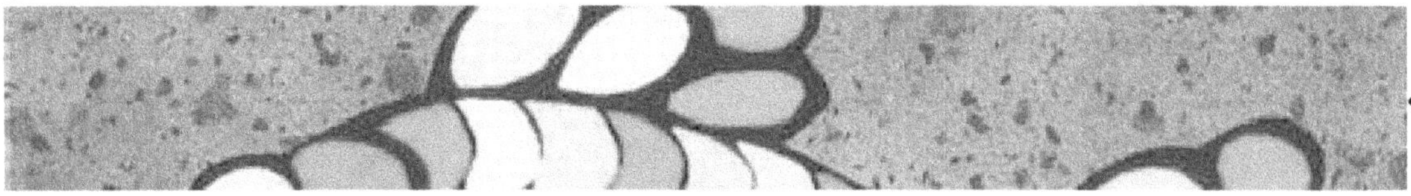

E 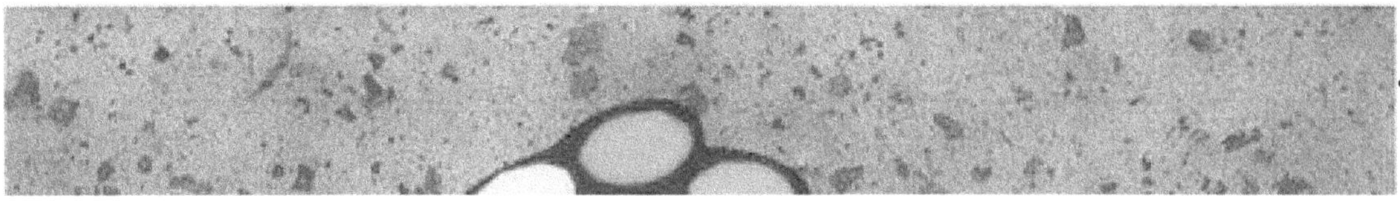

Color the Picture.

www.NolaTheNurse.com

Draw the missing picture in the given space.

Spot five differences between these two pictures.

Look at the filled boxes carefully and complete the patterns in the blank boxes.

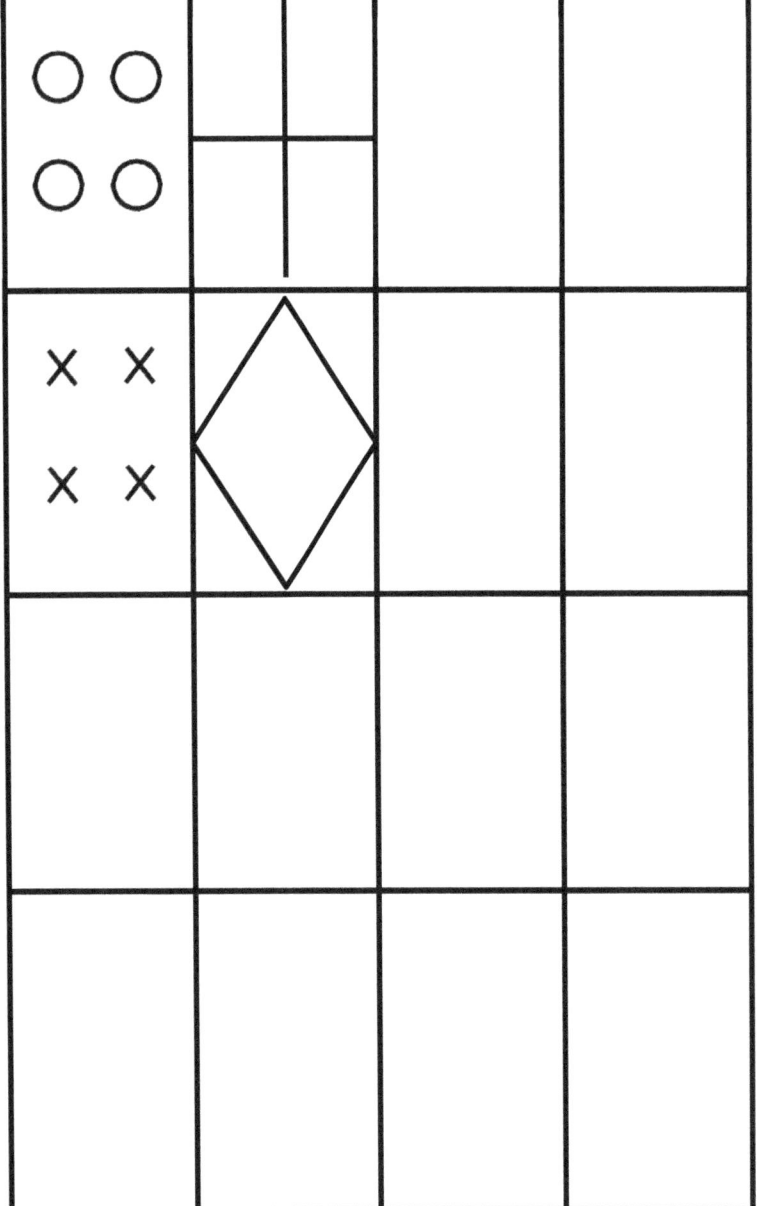

Charo The CRNA

Tick [✓] the two identical pictures.

www.NolaTheNurse.com

Join the dots from 1 to 30.

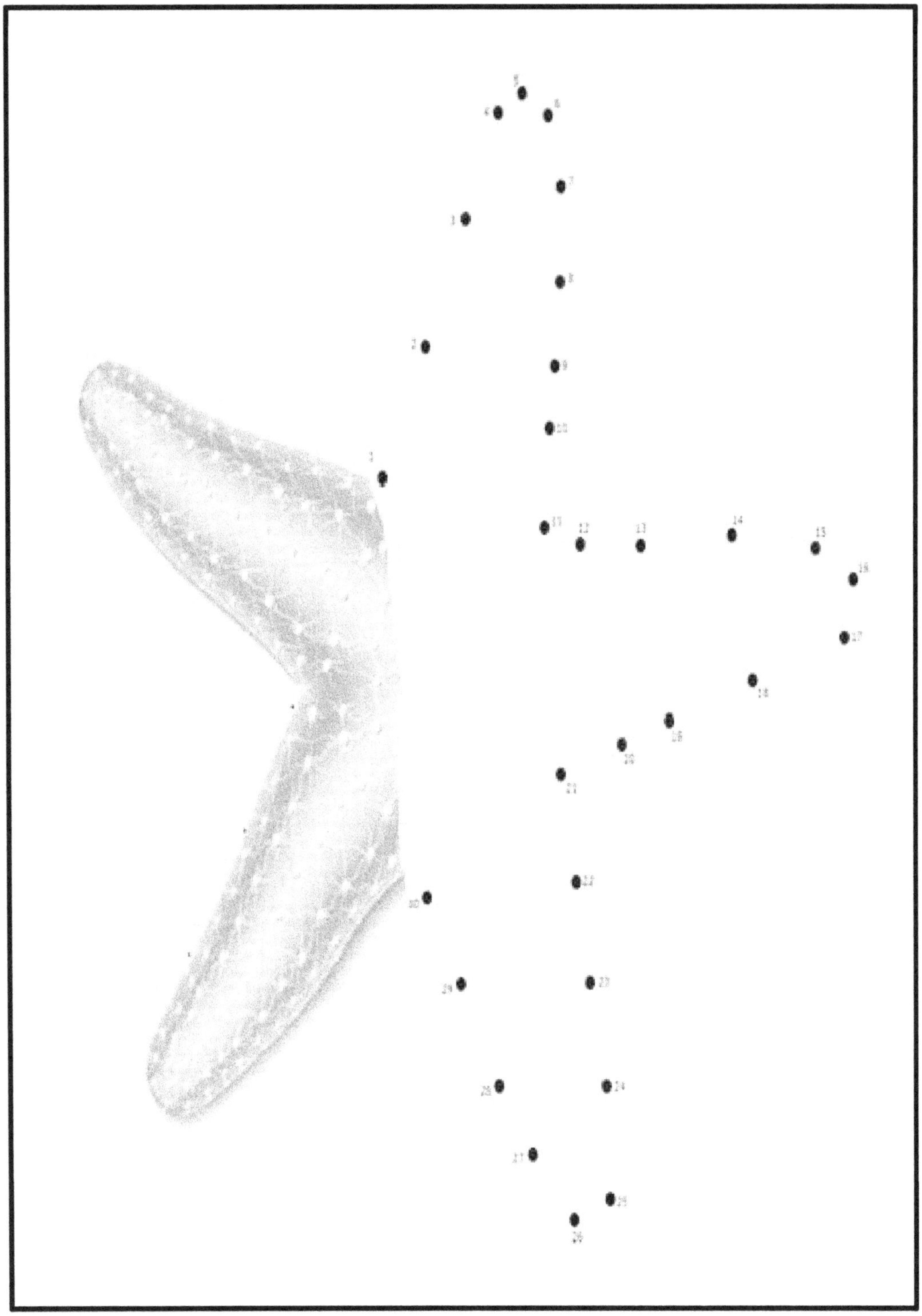

Cross [X] the odd one out.

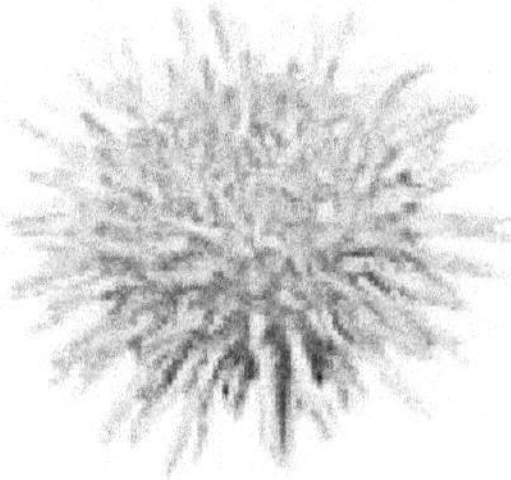

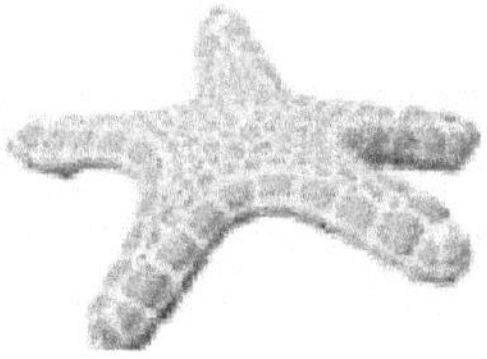

Draw the correct shapes to complete the patterns.

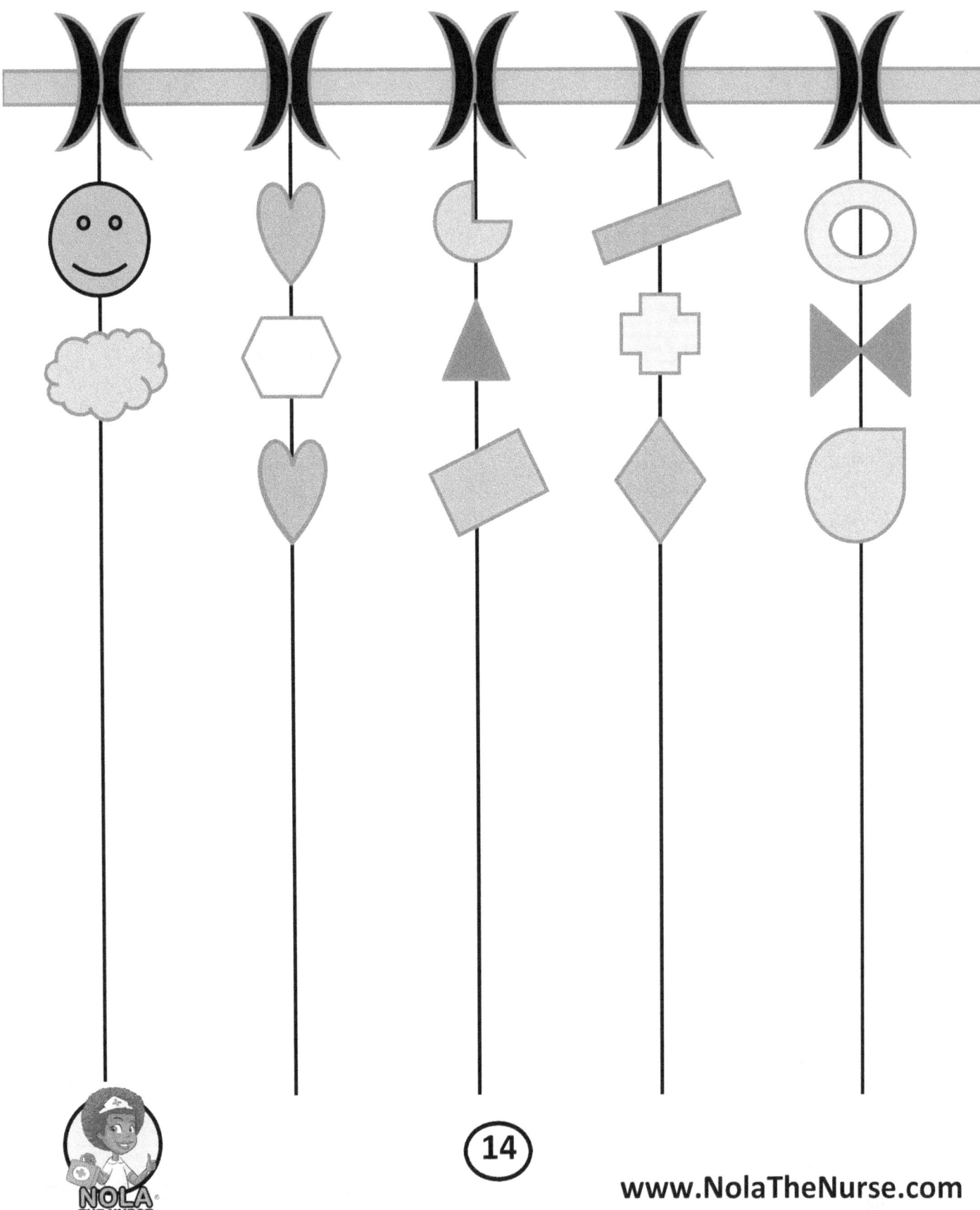

Write the first letter of each picture in the box and say aloud the name of the fruit in the picture.

Draw the picture in the enlarged grid.

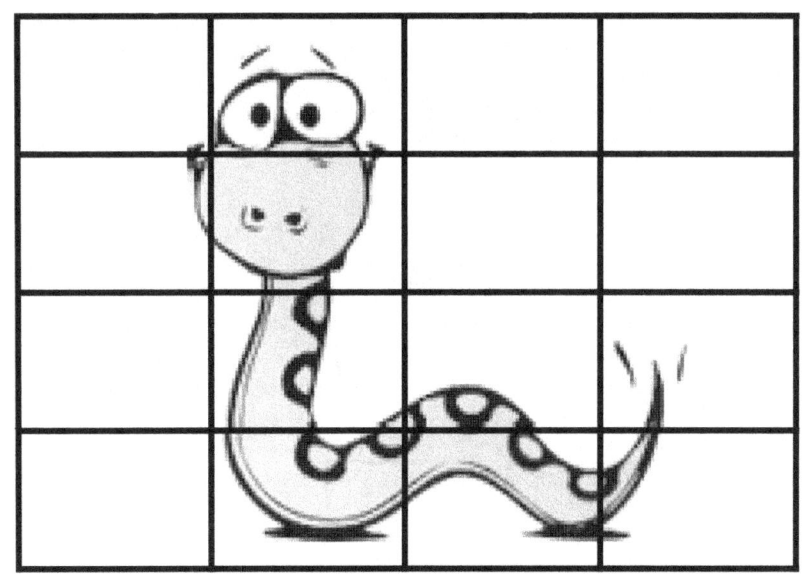

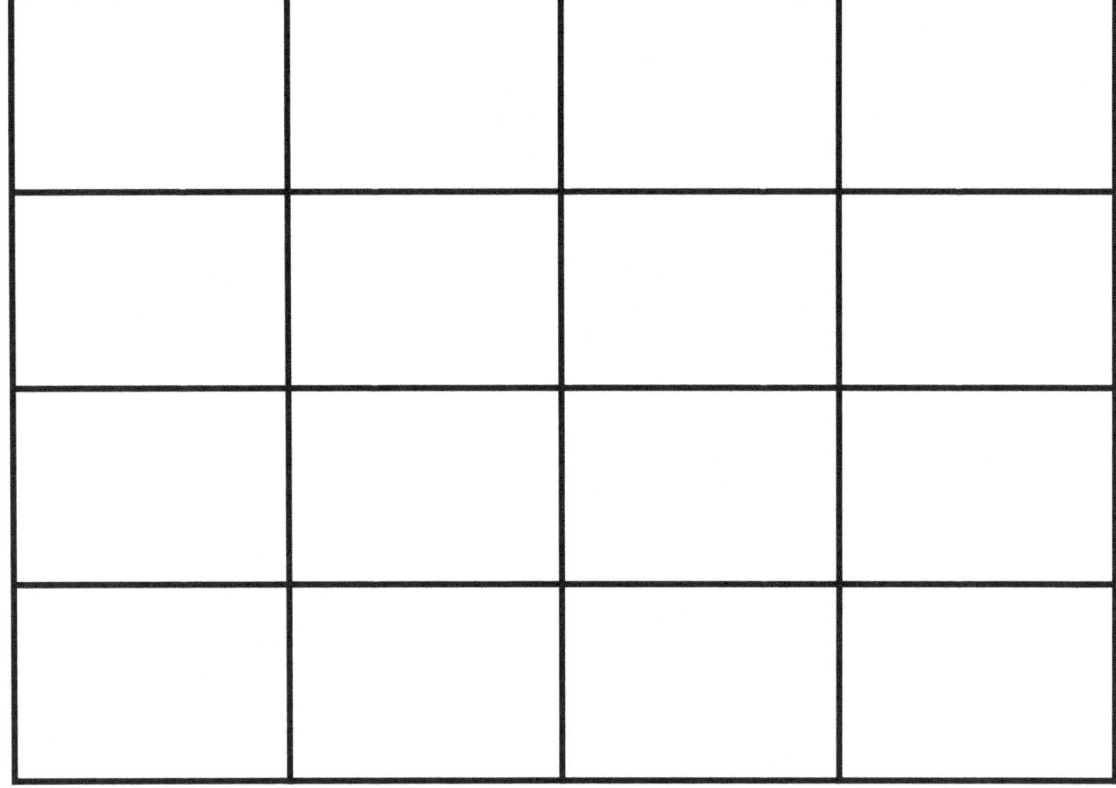

Match the picture to its correct outline.

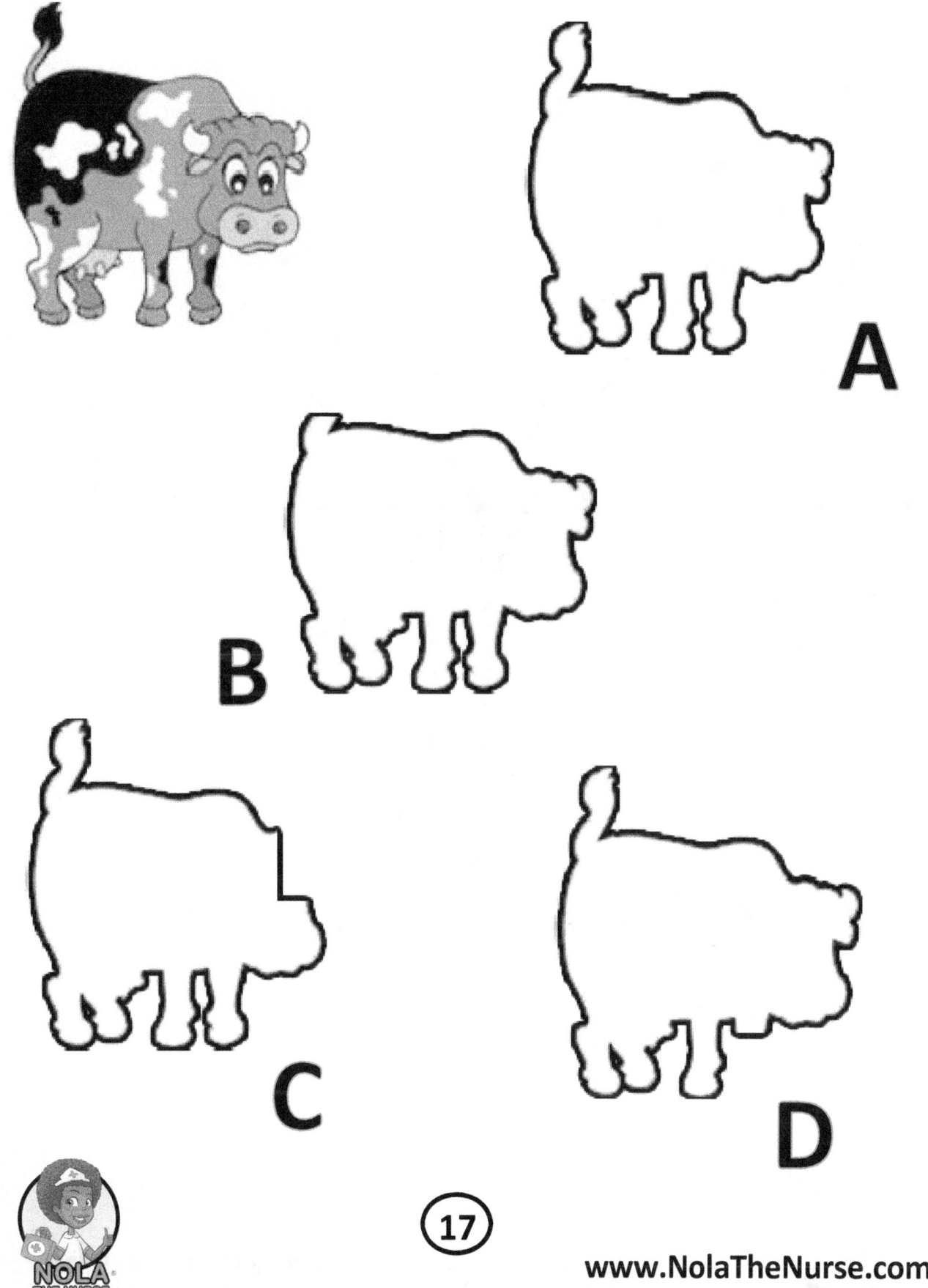

Color the picture.

www.NolaTheNurse.com

Rearrange the jumbled pieces of the given picture.

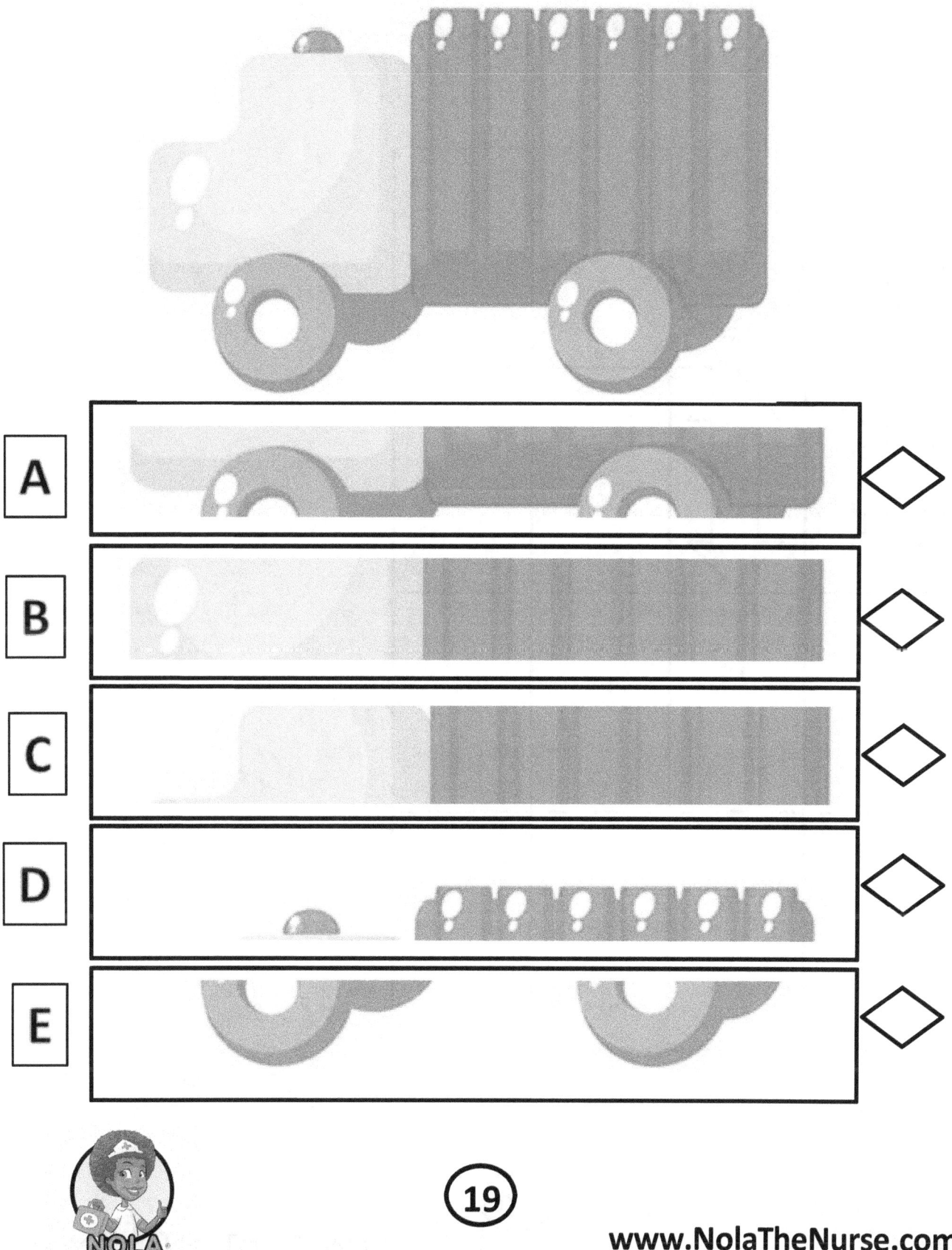

Look at the filled boxes carefully and complete the patterns in the blank boxes.

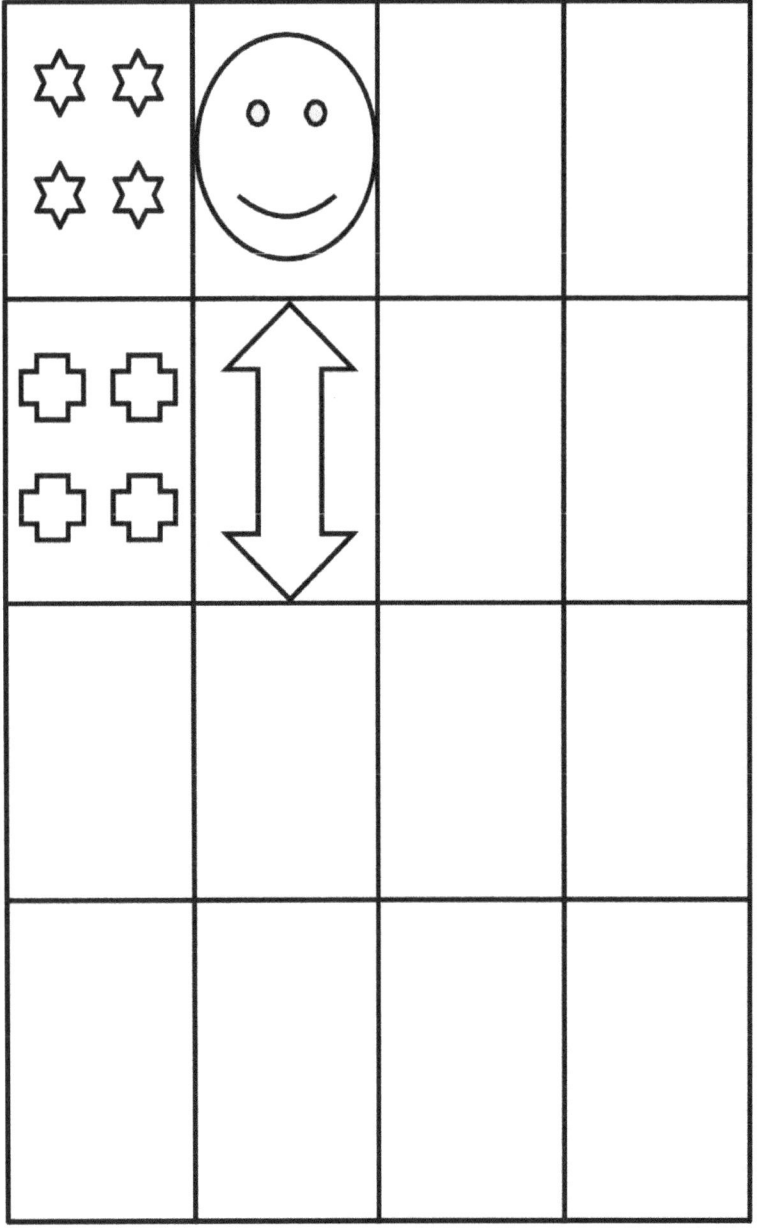

Bax The Nurse

www.NolaTheNurse.com

Make new words from the word Dinosaur and write in the dinosaur's body.

Dinosaur

www.NolaTheNurse.com

Draw the missing picture in the given space.

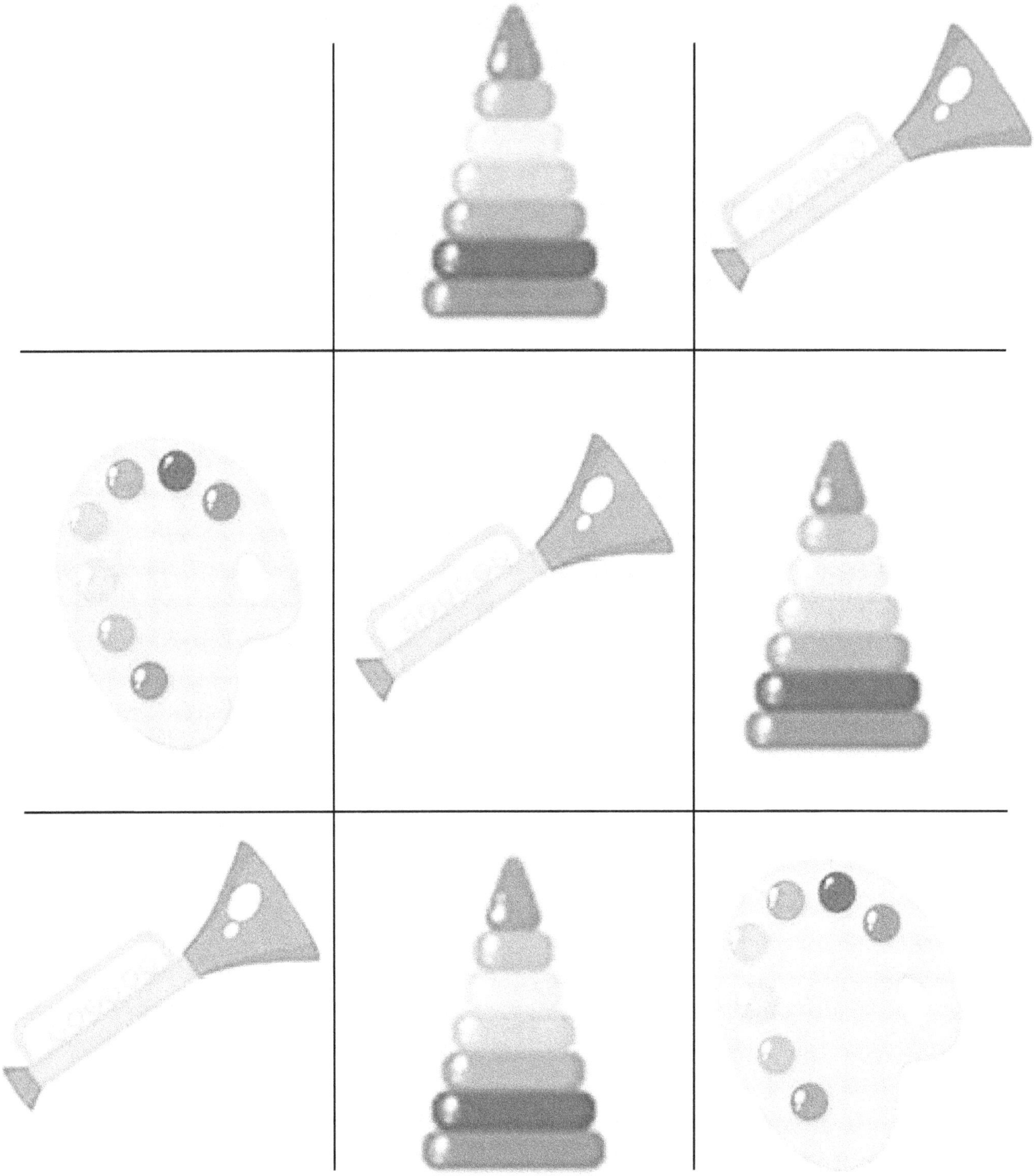

www.NolaTheNurse.com

Draw the picture in the enlarged grid.

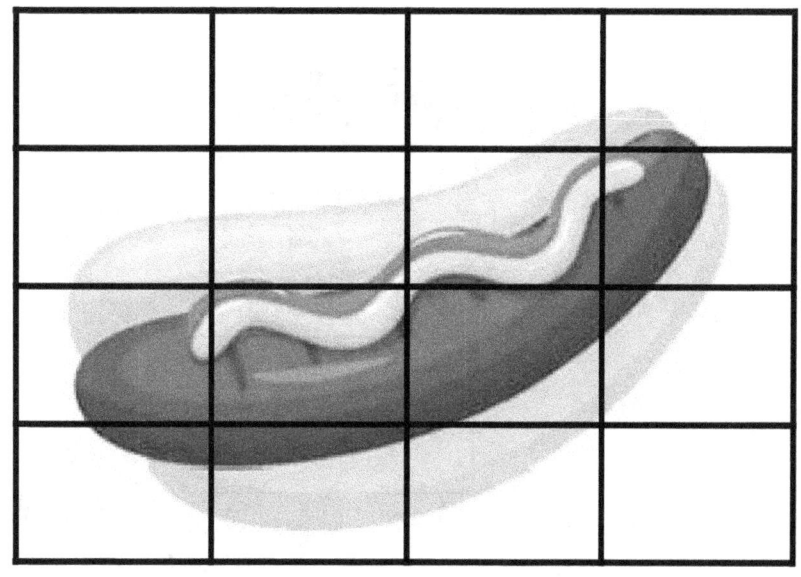

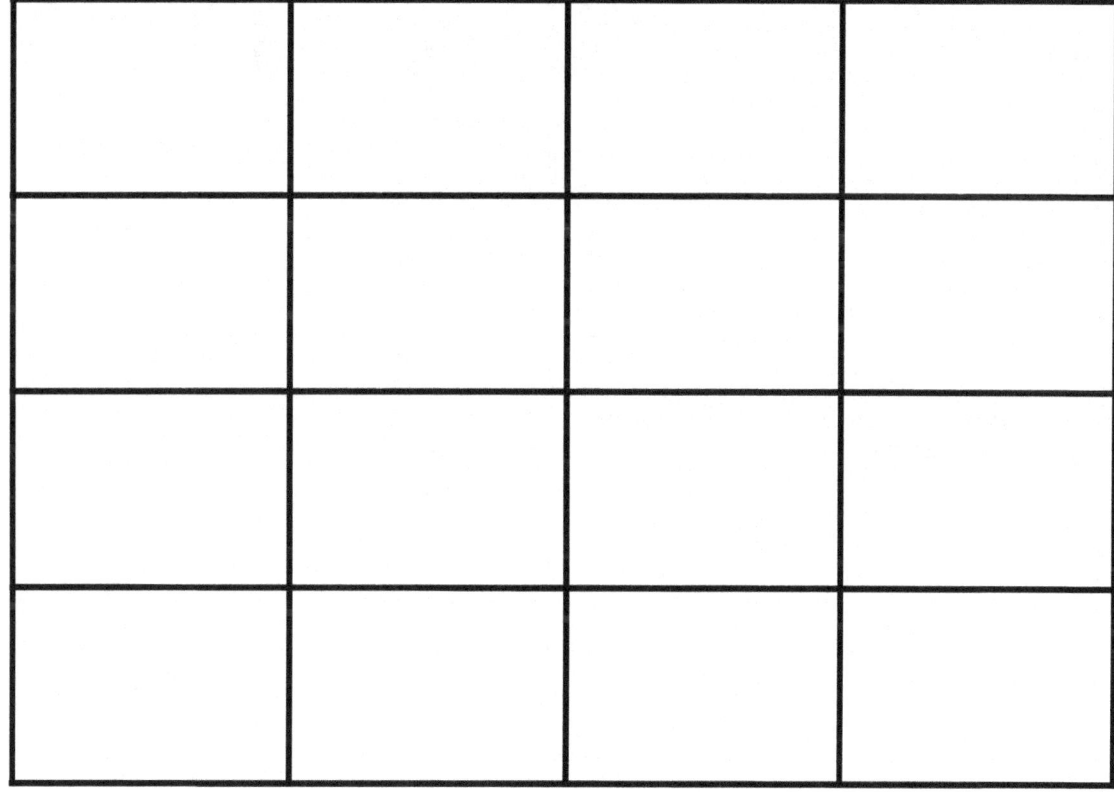

23

www.NolaTheNurse.com

Check [✓] the missing part...

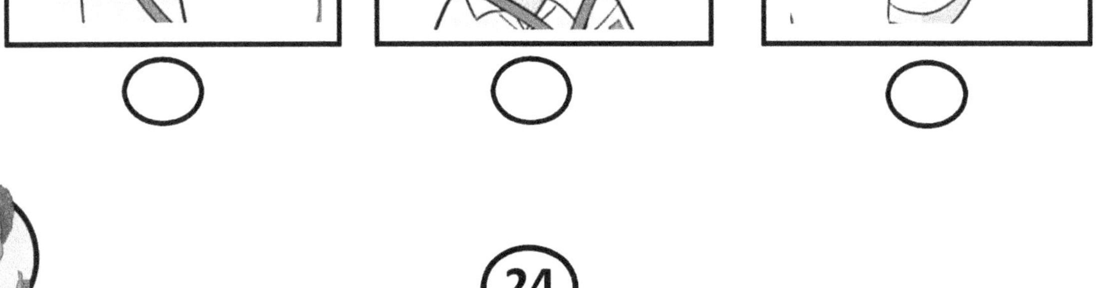

Check [✓] the two identical pictures.

Cross [X] the odd one out.

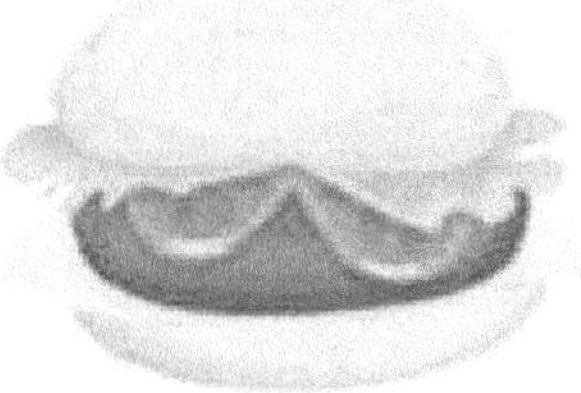

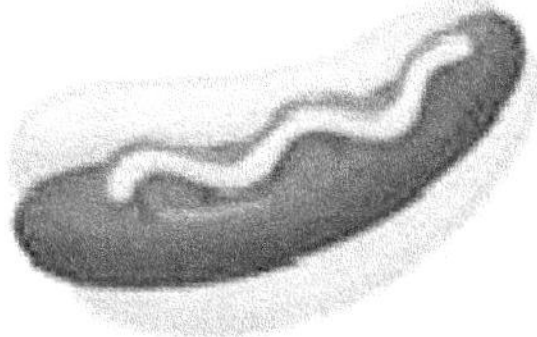

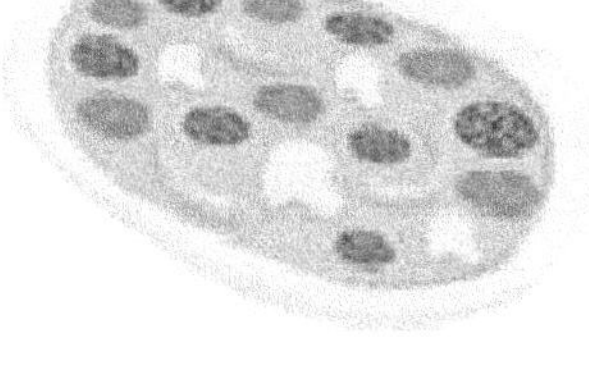

Write the first letter of each picture in the box and say aloud the name of the animal in the picture.

Join the dots and color the picture.

Match the picture to its correct outline.

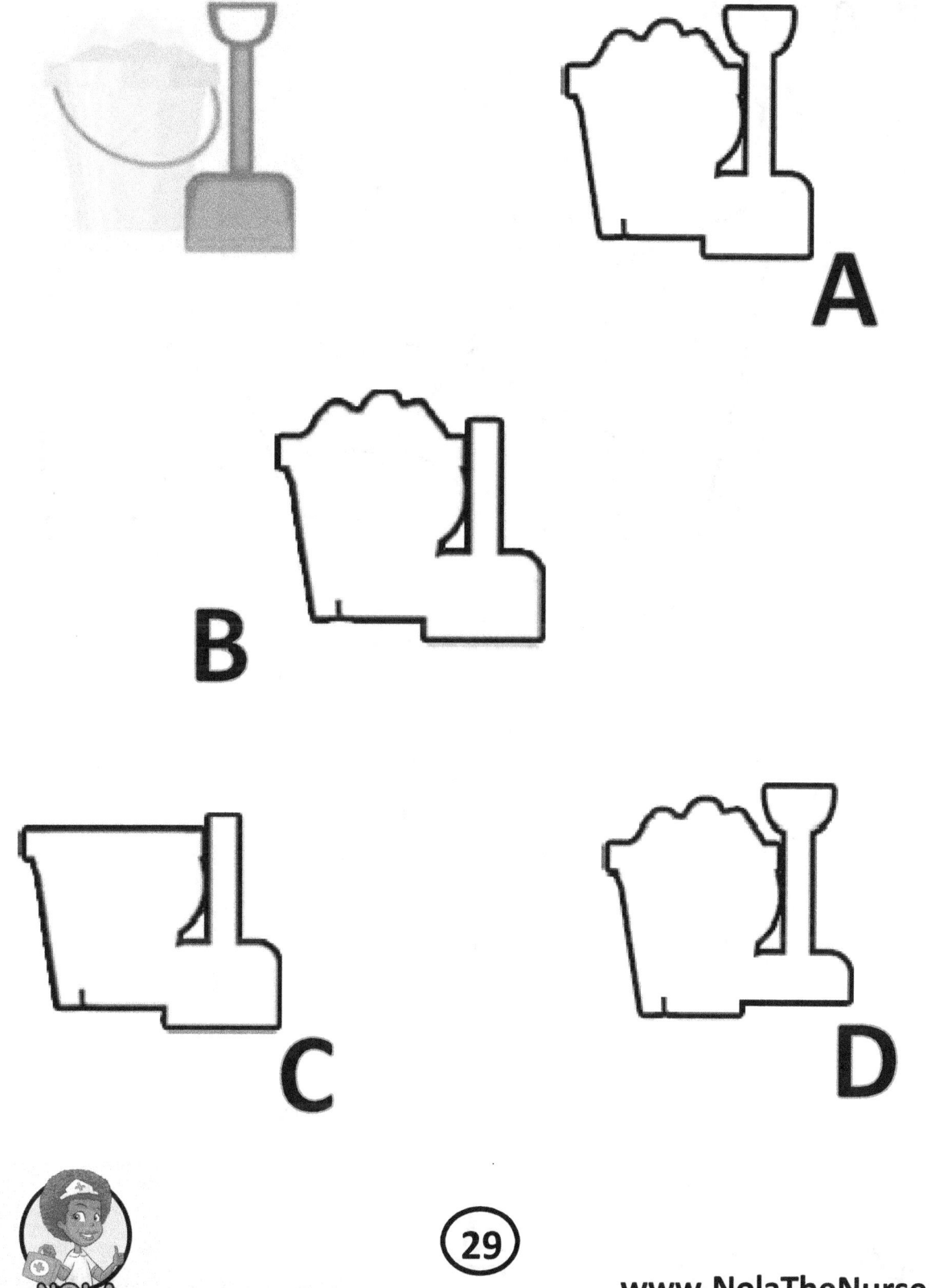

Help the cow to eat grass.

Make the picture by using the dots.

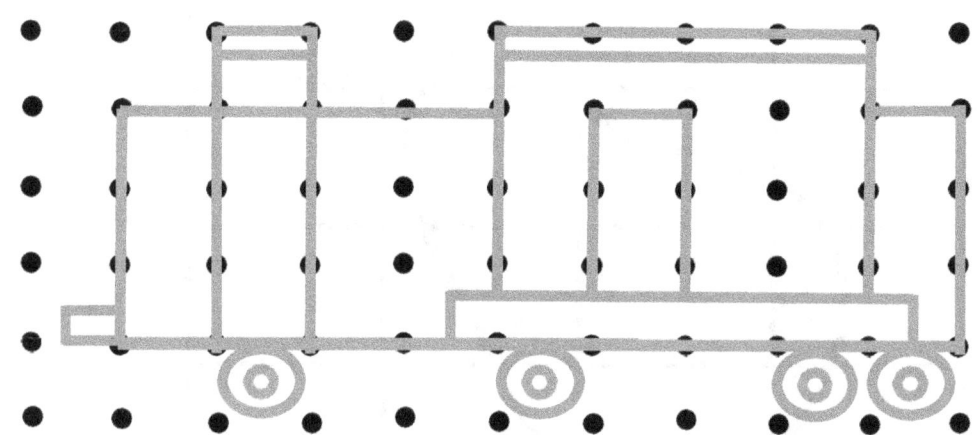

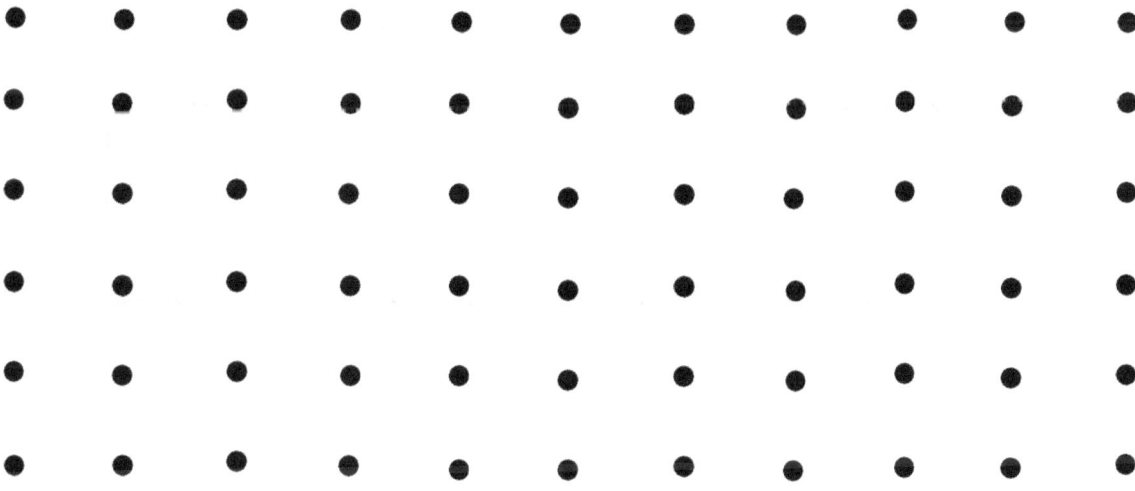

31

www.NolaTheNurse.com

Draw the picture in the enlarged grid.

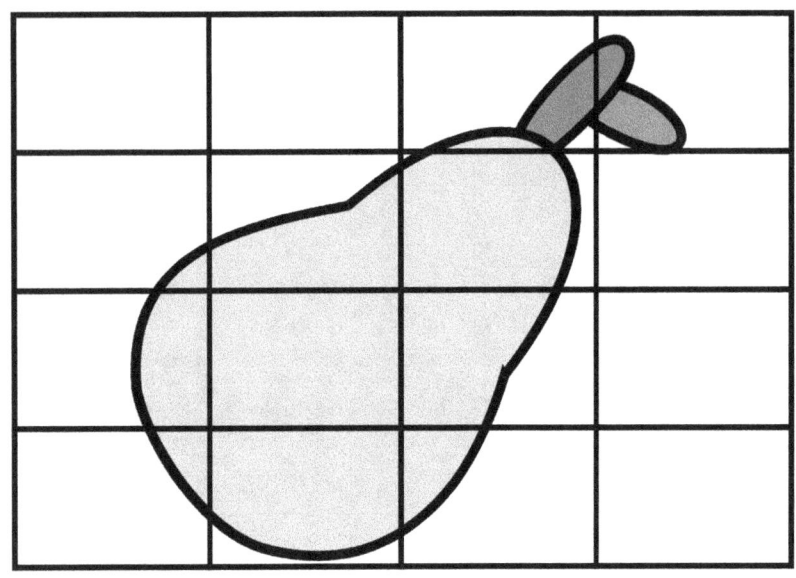

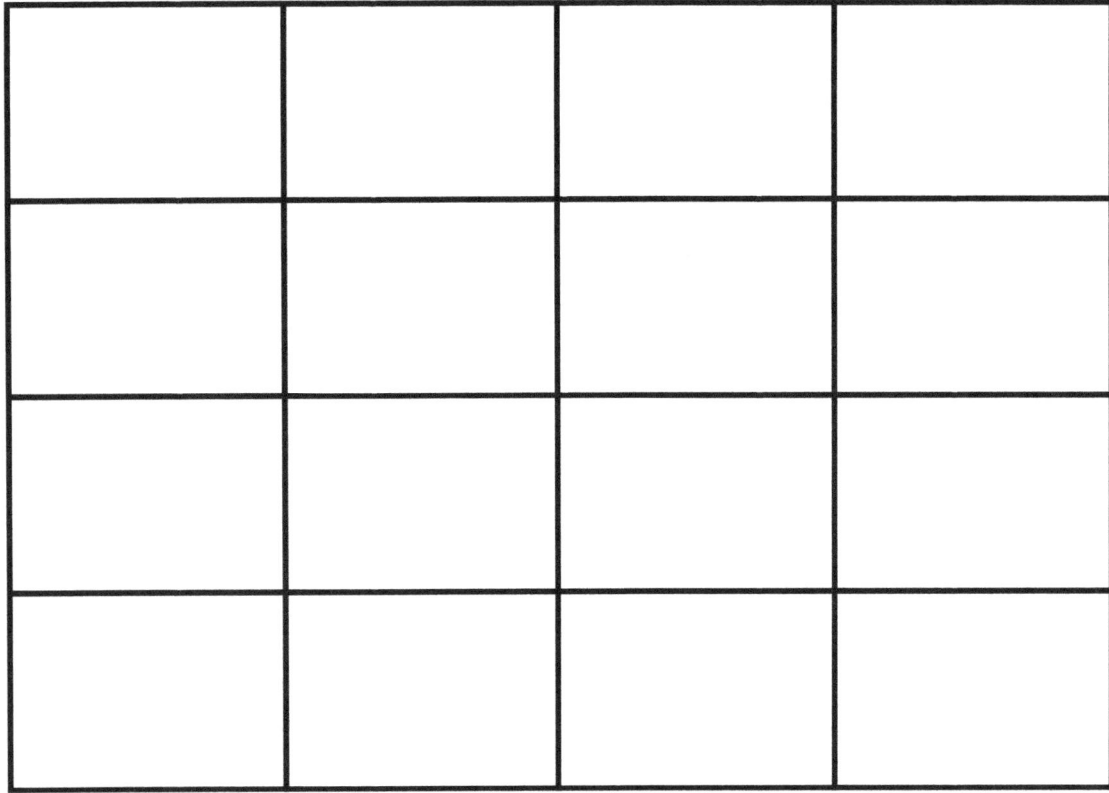

Use the object pictures to solve the puzzle.

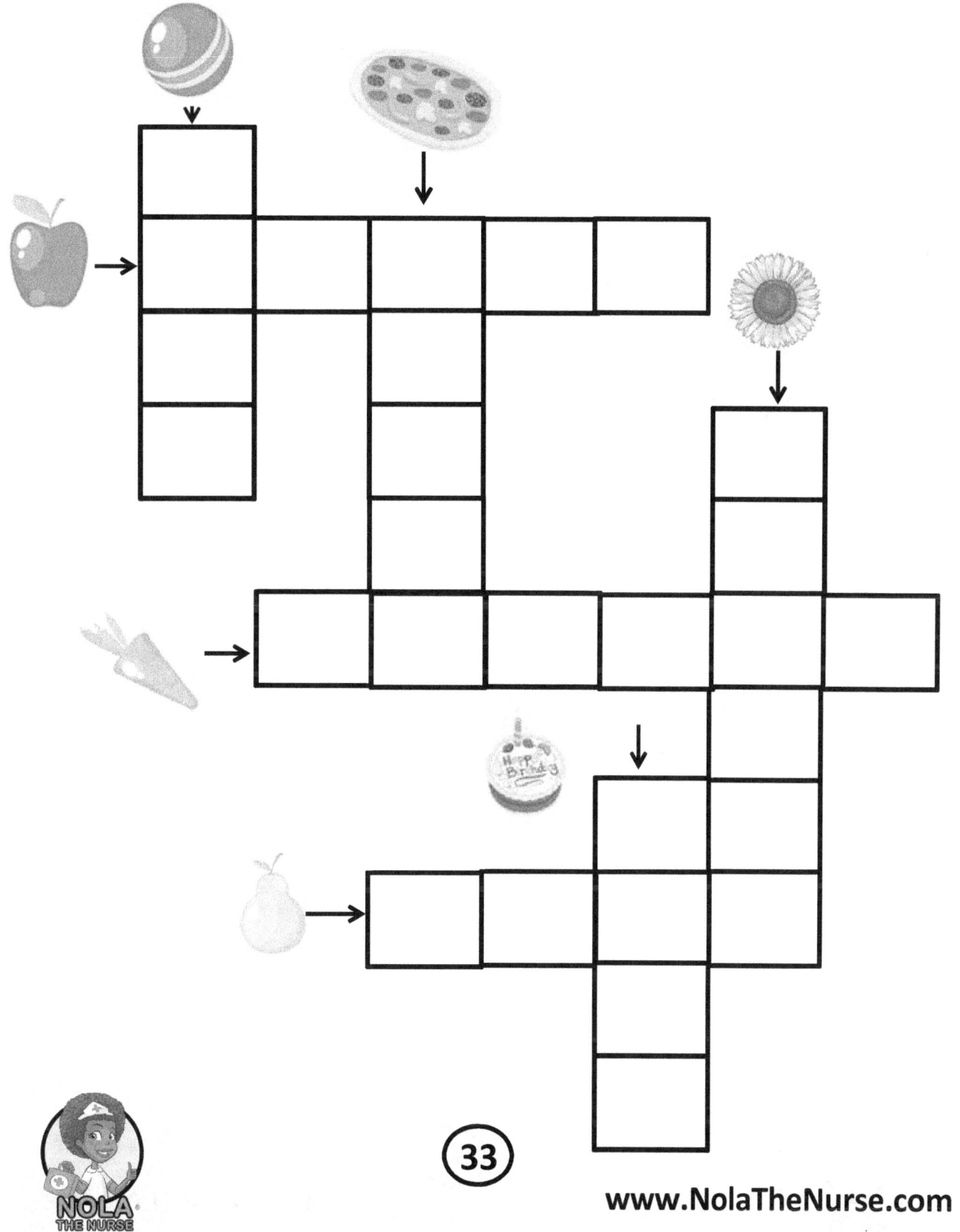

Write the correct beginning letter for the given object.

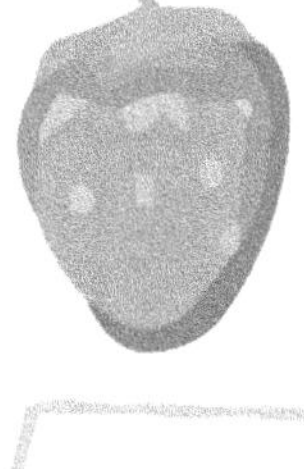

Help the lion to reach the den by joining the words ending with 'll'.

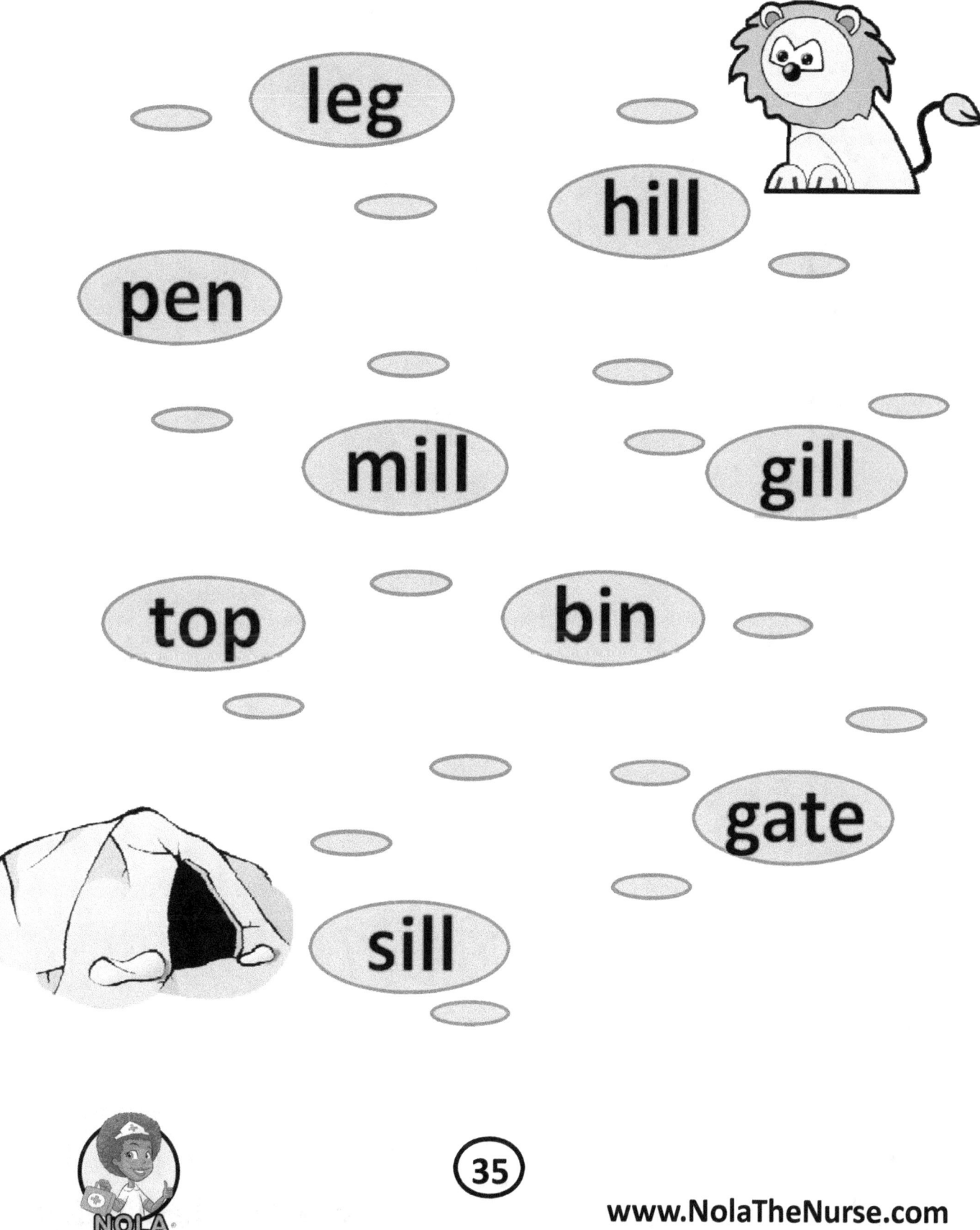

Circle the pictures that begin with the given letter sound.

A	apple	pyramid/top	truck
B	bug	top	ball
C	strawberry	cow	cake
D	drum	ice cream	duck
E	eggs in nest	candles	bear
F	pig	fish	fan

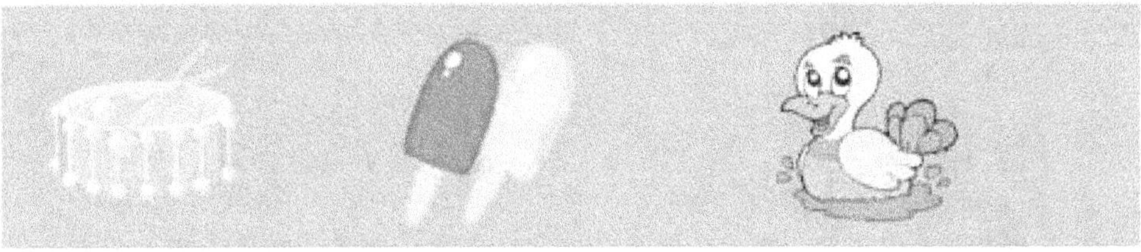

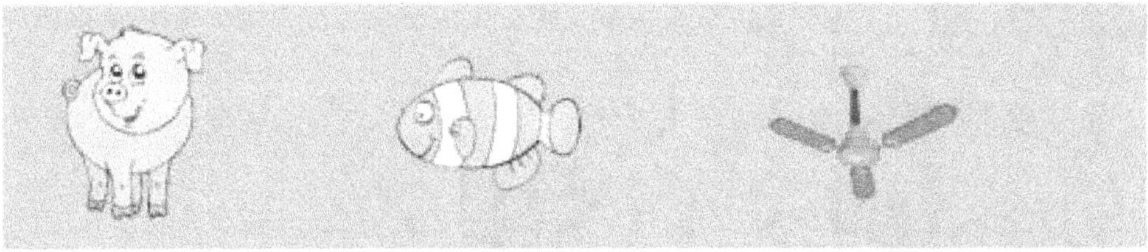

Given below are some objects. In-front of them are people using them. Match both of them correctly.

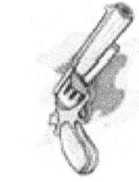

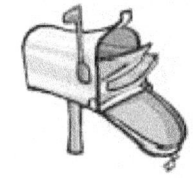

www.NolaTheNurse.com

Look at the given pictures and circle the things that can be eaten.

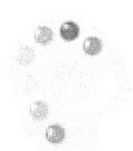

Match the animals with their names.

Pig

Dog

Cow

Sheep

Duck

www.NolaTheNurse.com

Look at the given pictures and circle the things that can be eaten.

 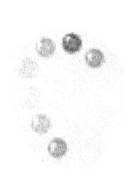

These following free color sheets are placed here to help you get to know the characters from the Nola The Nurse® children's book series. Enjoy and pick up a copy of the hottest selling children's book in America that was recently featured on The Harry Show!

Dr. Baker Nurse Practitioner

Gumbo

Adar

Nola The Nurse

Anita

Dr. Eden Nurse Practitioner

Maddi the Midwife

More books by Dr. Baker

Nola The Nurse® She's On The Go Series Vol 1
Nola The Nurse® & Friends Explore The Holi Fest She's On The Go Series Vol 2
Nola The Nurse® & Friends Explore The Holi Fest She's On The Go Series Vol 2 Coloring Book
Nola The Nurse® Remembers Hurricane Katrina Special Edition
Nola The Nurse® Remembers Hurricane Katrina Special Edition Coloring Book
Black Dot

Upcoming Titles:
Nola The Nurse® Activity Book for Kindergarten Vol 2
Nola The Nurse® Math Worksheets for Kindergarten Vol 3
Nola The Nurse® English/Sight Worksheets for Kindergarten Vol 4
Nola The Nurse® Math/English Worksheets for Preschoolers Vol 5
Nola The Nurse® Math Worksheets for First Graders Vol 6
Nola The Nurse® STEM Activity Book for 5-8 year olds Vol 7

www.NolaTheNurse.com
DrBaker@NolaTheNurse.com

About the Author

Dr. Scharmaine L. Baker, NP is a nationally recognized and award-winning nurse practitioner in New Orleans, Louisiana. She has received numerous honors and awards for her contributions to healthcare in New Orleans since she became a family nurse practitioner in 2000, including the 2013 Healthcare Hero award (New Orleans City Business magazine) and 2008 Entrepreneur of the Year award (ADVANCE for Nurse Practitioner magazine).

Dr. Baker has a doctor of nursing practice (DNP) degree from Chatham University in Pittsburgh, PA, and she is a fellow of the American Association of Nurse Practitioners (AANP). She was inspired to make house calls while caring for her grandmother, who was ill and needed an in-home doctor.

After Hurricane Katrina, Dr. Baker was instrumental in caring for the sick and disabled in New Orleans, where hospitals had closed and doctors had evacuated but never returned. Her patient load went from 100 to 500 in only three months. Thanks to her passion and unwavering dedication to caring for homebound patients in her home town, Dr. Baker's story was featured on the CBS Evening News with Katie Couric.

Today, Dr. Baker maintains a busy private practice in New Orleans by making house calls to the elderly and disabled who would otherwise not receive healthcare.

When this award-winning and nationally known nurse practitioner is not on the road delivering keynote speeches and attending various other media events, she loves reading to her children, Skylar Rose and Wyatt Shane.

www.DrBakerNP.com
www.NolaTheNurse.com
https://shop.nolathenurse.com

www.ingramcontent.com/pod-product-compliance
Lightning Source LLC
Chambersburg PA
CBHW081356080526
44588CB00016B/2515